The Qalam of Amir Khusro and His Perspectives on South Asian Heritage

By Aparna Joshi and Sapna Pandey

1

Table of Contents

Acknowledgment

We Would like to express our deep gratitude to our parents for providing us with a strong support system to explore the field of Amir Khusro's work and the world through our endless hours of research and writing processes.

Further, we would like to also extend our most sincere gratitude to our to the Faculty of the History Department at Kamala Nehru College, for being our guides through this long process of attempting to study primary sources, secondary sources, and the historiographical interpretations of these various elements which created the basis of this work.

We would lastly like to extend our gratitude to the various Librarians and library staff at the India International Center, Kamala Nehru College, Nehru

Memorial Museum and Library, and Delhi Gymkhana

Club for assisting us with finding the various primary

and secondary materials that helped us shape this thesis.

Prologue

Recent studies in the concept of historiography and History writing reveal a rough and absolute distribution of texts into three phases, the pre historical, proto historical and historical. With this classification, they aimed to negate various sources as merely mythological with each period and propagate others as expressions of scientific history writing.

However, the earliest roots of the Islamic historical writing in India can be seen as an import of the Arabic influence seen during the phase of the Delhi Sultanate. The Arabic style of History writing as pointed out by Ira Lapidus was heavily reliant on the depiction and relaying of 'facts' or Ijaz, it has been considered by scholars scientific miracles.

These miracles, however, could be assimilated in the text as Hadith or real-life instances only after being recounted by several people and being placed in a historical timeline after the adoption of the lunar or Hijri calendar. The style of writing, therefore, was driven by fact, or by an eyewitness account.

This style was adopted and used by the Early Islamic Caliphate to gain legitimacy by recording and reporting facts. However, in the second Ummayat caliphate, the emphasis shifted from merely reporting facts to the process of gaining legitimacy and power through the creation of genealogies and the medium of literature at large.

This process led to the development of the more ornamental 'Persianate' historiography, a style of writing which was also adopted by the Sultans of Delhi, who saw themselves as the representatives of the Caliphate in India. They also drew inspiration from the mythology associated with the Prophet.

Islamic Historiography in India, has further taken shape in four distinct phases. The earliest form of historical sources in India from the period of the Sultanate was based on the Quran and primarily, this can be further classified as the biographical texts known as the Sira or the Magazhi, which informed the reader about the familial background of the Prophet Muhammad. It was from texts such as these that later historians such as Firdausi and Barani began to connect the Sultanate system to the Islamic method of Governance, an idea which was propounded in the text of the Padshahnameh.

Another classification of Islamic sources found in India was the Tawarikh (plural for the term Tarikh) translated to mean ' history or recounted events'. The Tarikh form of history writing was propagated by the later Sultans.

A defining feature of the Tarikh tradition as it developed on the South Asian Sub-continent under the patronage of the Delhi Sultans was the adoption of an ornate linguistic form as pointed out by Francesca Orsini.

The Tarikh generally laid emphasis on the politico-military campaigns and the nature of a military state as opposed to the condition of the social fabric of the period. This becomes evident in the writing of Mahmud of Ghazni's Tarikh recounted by Ya'ub Bin Ali Lais. Another source used to recount Islamic history on the subcontinent in a period later than the Delhi Sultans were the Insha texts, which relied heavily on the nature of hierarchy and administration as was visible in contemporary state formations.

Richard Eaton however, using the region of Bijapur as a case study on the Khanqah system points out a distinctive teaching-learning process that was based on the Pir and Murid concept of passing esoteric and mystical knowledge, however, in distinction to the indigenously prevalent system of knowledge passing which was based on caste purity, this system was based on the capability of the Murid.

Therefore, the types of sources in Sufi literature were a combination of historical and mystical sources. Amir Khusro further developed other types of texts in the form of poetry which came to be categorized in the form of classical literature at the time, this writing was a scathing commentary on the political system of the period as well as a biting social commentary of the individual's experience in Sultanate reign.

The proceedings of the Sufi Khanqah can be reconstructed using the Malfuzat texts, which were primarily the collection of discourses by the Pir to their Murids. The spoken word in the Majlis (Public Gathering) was recounted by the disciples in the form of a dialogue. A Malfuzat provides contemporary historians with a lens into the state and Khanqah relationship or that of the equation between the two.

Masnavi texts are another form of the literature identified with the Sufi Khanqah, these texts are long narrative poems, which are not merely about characters rather they paint an accurate image of particular historical events and moments of relevance seen in the past. Scholars of contemporary Sufism tend to link the art of Masnavi composition with Middle-Eastern Mystic and Saint Jalaluddin Rumi, however, in the Indian Subcontinent, the art of Masnavi was popularised by Amir Khusro. He also diverged from the tradition of composing Masnavi in pure Persian instead opting for what would later be termed as Hindawi.

Prem Akhyan Literature has also been identified with the Sufi Khanqah and Sufi traditions. It was Richard Eaton who suggested that it was the vernacular nature of the prem Akhyan which was instrumental in the development of Sufi Silsilahs in India.

Eaton draws upon the Prem Akhyan written by Malik Muhammad Jayasi to prove that it was the imagery introduced in the Prem Akhyan which allowed for the text to have a popular appeal.

The Sufi order within Islam is seen to have a direct lineage to the prophet Muhammad himself. It was seen as a path of self-discovery, moving away from the traditional orders of Islam (Sunni and Shia) which as pointed out by Ira Lapidus had developed a ritualistic practice, which was further constricted by the Ummayat. However, the development of Sufi Islam itself did not develop as a uniform practice within its fold, several opinions created the Sufi orders as either Besharia (opposed to traditional sharia law) or Basharia (in keeping with Sharia Law). In the Indian subcontinent, we see an onset of two Basharia sects and three Besharia orders of Sufism. The Basharia sects prevalent in India were the Nashqbandi and Qadri, Suhurawardi were orthodox in their outlook towards Islam, therefore, moved away from adapting to the regional practices.

The three Besharia orders included the Rishi sect, which developed out of the practice of Shaivism in the Northern Part of India (Jammu and Kashmir), another element was the Sufis of the Deccan were the development of the Ghazis, as pointed out by Peter Jackson.

However, the most powerful sect of the Sufis with pan-India popularity was the Chishti Sufi Silsilah. The Chishti order is named after Chisht, a town in Khurasan. Chisti and the Suhrawardi silsilahs were popular during the phase of the Delhi Sultanate period. The Suhrawardis were active in Punjab and Sindh while the Chishti's were active in Delhi, Rajasthan, and other parts of the western

Gangetic plains. By the end of the sultanate period, Chisti had spread to the eastern regions of the Gangetic plain (Bihar and Bengal) and into the Deccan.

In India, this order was established by Muinuddin Chishti. He seems to have moved into India after the invasion of Muhammad Ghori and subsequently to Ajmer in 1206. The fame of Khwaja Moinuddin grew after his death in 1235.

The presence of this order was established by Qutbuddin Bakhtiyar Kaki. The Chishti order laid great emphasis on the simplicity of life, poverty, humility, and selfless devotion to God.

They regarded the renunciation of worldly possessions as necessary for the control of the senses that were necessary to maintain a spiritual life. They refused any grants from the state or sultans for their maintenance.

however, it has been a topic of debate amongst various historians who not only talk about the Sufis but the kind of nature of the relationship between the Sufis and chisti pirs. Nizamuddin Auliya, who is seen as the was the best-known Chishti saint of the Sultanate period, lived in the fourteenth century, during a period of political change and turmoil.

The khanqah of Nizamuddin Auliya's emerged as an important center of the training of the Sufis where almost all the political authorities used to visit the shrine to seek the blessings of the saints. However, the Khwaja is said to have maintained a strict policy of not involving himself in the political domains of the sultans and other many respects. Nasiruddin Chiragh Dehlavi was another of the Chishti saints of Delhi. He played an active role in the political affairs of the period. All these enabled Sufis to maintain a loyal and dedicated following. We have numerous pieces of evidence which show that there had been a great interest among the Indian Sufis to study and understand the Hindu mystical ideas. There are also examples of the adaptation of the practices of Hindu Jogis.

By the 13th century, we see the emergence of the Chishti Order in the Deccan which was established by Shaikh Burhanuddin Gharib, and between the 14th and 16th centuries, many Chishti Sufis migrated to Gulbarga.

Richard Eaton has elaborated on how this has coincided with a change in nature where some of the Chishti began accepting grants and patronage from the ruling establishment and some also became landowners.

Muhammad Banda Nawaz is among the famous pirs in the region. The city of Bijapur emerged as an important center for Sufi activity.

The Man Introduced

Amir Khusrau was born at Patiali in district Etah of U.P. in 1252. Although Amīr Khusrau included much autobiographical information in his writings, the details of his origins are not clear. His father was Saifuddīn Shamsī, who is said to have migrated from Central Asia, and was married to the daughter of Imād al-Mulk, an Indian Muslim.

He was the disciple of famous Sufi saint Nizamuddin Auliya. Khusrau is regarded as one of the greatest Persian poets and historians of his age. He was popularly known as Tuti-Hind "The parrot of India". His contribution to the development of the Gazal was significant. Khusrau is credited for the invention of the Sitar.

Amir Khusroo had written a historical Masnavi Nuh-Siphr on the name of Qutub-ud-din son of Alauddin Khilji. In Nuh-Sipihr, he claimed that- "I saw whatever I see with my own eyes – not stories or tales of the past". His ethics of writing are best illustrated by his remarks in his short Masnavi Miftah-Al Futa.

He is one of the most celebrated poets of medieval India, writing both in Persian, and Hindavī. Generally, he is seen as a court noble, an Sūfī mystic, an extensive traveler, and a poet. Every aspect has its role to play in his composition. But we must also look at another less explored identity of Khusrau, as the Historian. He had claimed in Nūh Sipihr, "I say whatever I see with my own eyes – not stories or tales of the past." his ethics of writing are best illustrated by his remarks in his short masnavī9, Miftāh-al-Futūh.

Khusrau's major works include his five dīwāns- Tuhfat al-Sighar (poems of adolescence), Baqiyya-Yi-Naqiyya, Nihāyat al-Kamāl; etc.

His masnavīs, as many historians observe, offer insight into more than just history. The most important work is Qirān al-Sadain (conjunction/meeting of two planets). It is written in Persian and includes ghazals. Its main theme is the meeting and the conflict (and its resolution) between BughraKhān and his son, Sultān Muīzzuddīn Kaiqubād. Besides that, Khusrau also gives information about the army, the climate in Awadh, and the description of the city of Delhi.

Khusrau's works become handy as far as the factual information with historical relevance is concerned. The later historian Baranī quotes Khusrau on many occasions to confirm some of the major points of view on past events. In many works, Barani's assertion was supplemented by the facts furnished by Amīr Khusrau.

Peter Hardy does not consider him a historian, positing that he lacks them and chronology. To Hardy, "Khusrao wrote about the past to fulfill not a practical, or a moral or a religious or an academic purpose, but to fulfill an aesthetic purpose."

Many scholars and critics acknowledge] Khusro as a historian because of the historical documentation he did in his writings. Though there is debate whether Khusro can be called a historian. His works are symbols of the

cross-cultural aesthetics of literature and music.

His Plume: The Creator of Qawwali

Amir Khusro has a unique identity among the Sufis of Delhi, however, his life continues to intrigue historians and scholars, due to its diverse nature and the lack of information about him. This is because Amir Khusro's correspondence with his Spiritual master Nizamuddin Auliya was buried with him, six months after the death of his Master.

Amir Khusro, however, lives on in the hearts and minds of modern-day followers of the Chisti Silsila and its believers. This is because he is believed to have introduced Qawwali, a form of mystical singing and chanting (zikr) to reach the state of oneness (fannah) with God, often expressed as Sanam. His spiritual journey can be traced through four distinct qawwali composed in various dialects used in Delhi.

Under the Microscope: A few Examples

Case Study 1: Rang

The Qawwali Rang was popularized by Nusrat Fateh Ali Khan, in 1985. Aaj Rang Hai, is a conversation between Amir Khusro and his mother, upon finding his spiritual master Nizamuddin Auliya.

The story goes, that Amir Khusro, was not a spiritually awakened child, ie, he did not particularly believe in the ideas of Sufism and a pir. His mother, on the contrary, had immense faith in Sufism and instructed him to bow before Nizamuddin Auliya.

He refused and said that if this man was Mehboob e Ilahi (a lover of God), then he will hear the 'Sher' (

poem/chaupai) that I recite in my heart and send me a response, after which I will truly believe I his powers. The poem that Amir Khusro recited was as follows:

" Kabutar Aaya jo tere darr Bana baaz ae shah, tune di kya mujhe awaz hai"

To this, the response that came was:

" Kya aap Turk hai, jo Janta hai sach wo Mera hamraz hai, nada hai wo, jisko iss dar se aitraz hai"

Roughly translated, the first sher talks about the unknowing soul represented by the pigeon wh with divine knowledge is turned into an eagle signifying fearlessness and spiritual independence. On hearing this poem, Nizamuddin Auliya is said to have responded, that he who knows the truth, is my successor. He is a Turk, who does not believe in the power of this khanqah. This leaves Amir Khusro stunned, who then enters the khanqah and sees a divine glow on the face of Nizamuddin Auliya. On returning from the Khanqah, he tells his mother:

" माटी के तुम दीवरे

जो सुनियो हमरी बात

आज मिला वरा मोहे पिया का

जो जगियो सारी रात"

Amir Khusro aims to show how sudden his contact with his spiritual master turns out to be, it was as if the walls of the Khanqah had heard his poem to make him meet his spiritual master. Whom he describes as his 'Piya' (lover) and this revelation has led Nizamuddin Auliya to his successor, a concern that led him (Nizamuddin Auliya) sleepless nights. Amir Khusro goes on to tell his mother:

"आज रंग है री माँ रंग है री

आज रंग है री माँ रंग है री

आज रंग है री माँ रंग है री

आज रंग है री माँ रंग है री

मोरे ख्वाजा के घर रंग है री"

He expresses to his mother that today is an auspicious day, in his life and that of his Khwaja (teacher), upon finding the ideal teacher for him (Murshid) and finding the ideal student as his spiritual successor (Murid) for his teacher. He then goes on to tell his mother that this spiritual awakening is a result of her devotion and prayers to the Rasool (messenger of God) and that he has had a first-hand spiritual experience with his Khwaja Nizamuddin Auliya.

He has, however, already had exposure to the tradition of the Sufis in the earlier phase of his life under the influence of Mai Sahiba, Bibi Zulekha, the Mother of Nizamuddin Auliya. He pledges allegiance to the Sufi order and claims to serve the Sufi order for the remainder of his life.

This emotion is expressed in the following lines:

"रैनी चडी रसूल की

सो रंग मा लागे हाथ

जाका जोड़ा रंग दियो

सो धन धन वाके भाग"

In the subsequent few paragraphs, Amir Khusro goes on to repeat the name of God (Bismillah-i-Rehman Rahim Or lines from the Quran, from surahs initially placed as

these, are lines about the creation of the world in the
Cosmic reality) and his Murshid (Yah Nizamuddin
Auliya), as a form of zikr, in a drut (fast) tempo.

After this, he returned to describing his journey to the
pir, he says that he looked around the world for his
spiritual master, along with his mother before finding the
Khanqah of Nizamuddin Auliya, in Delhi.

Amir Khusro says that it was the radiance and simplicity
of the Khwaja that allowed him to be accepted as a
Murid. He says that his fortune will remain positive so
long as he is associated with the Pir, thus, giving him the
status of a God, in his life. This finds expression in the
following lines of Aaj Rang Hai:

"देश विदेश में ढूंड फिरी हूं

तोरा रंग मन भयो निजाम-ओ-द्दीन

तोरा रंग मन भयो निजाम-ओ-द्दीन

तोरा रंग मन भयो निजाम-ओ-द्दीन

Amir Khusro points out that he would be pulled back to the Khanqah of his Pir, irrespective of where he is, thus, alluding to the fact that he was a trader by profession and often traveled to several locations.

Mehru Jaffer points to a particular instance in the life of Amir Khusro, where he returned to the Khanqah and it is believed that Nizamuddin Auliya predicted losses for Khusro which then came true, making him a believer in the power of the Sufi Mystic.

खुसरो रेन सुहाग की

सो में जागी पी के संग

तन मोरा मन भी होगा

सो दोनों एक ही रंग रे

मेतो ऐसो रंग

हो महबूब-ए-ईलाही

मेतो ऐसो रंग"

He then goes on to describe his journey to various pilgrimage spots associated with both Islam and Hinduism such as Vrindavan and Mathura along with Basra however, in vain. Lastly, Amir Khusro in the song gives the listeners a brief insight into the history of the Chishti Silsila, beginning from Moinuddin Chishti, moving down to Baba Fariduddin Ganj e Shakar, Qutubuddin Bakhtiar Kaki, and Nizamuddin Auliya, his Pir.

In the second stage of his spiritual journey, he comes under the influence of the mother of Nizamuddin Auliya, Mai Sahiba Bibi Zuekha.

He writes several Ghazals in her honor, establishing her among the leading women Sufis of the time including

Rabia of Basra and Bibi Fatima Sam. Of these two Ghazals are particularly important. Amir Khusro though celebrated for his contribution to Qawwalis as a text and compositions. However, he also gained popularity by creating Ghazals, this was a compilation of 'sher', usually of the length of four to six stanzas which were popularised in post-Abbasid Arabia.

They depicted within themselves the high of the Arabic language and Persianate sophistication. Typically, there are two forms that a Ghazal may take in this period. One form was that which transcended human love and depicted the emotion of Ishq Haqiqi while the other belonging to the shringaric type of literature, praised the beloved. However, these two types of Ghazals often overlapped or came in contact with each other.

They were further less structured than the presentation of the Qawwali, these could be sung outside the confines of the Majlis and were often sung in the female voice by male singers.

This reflected the perception of openness about the expression of feelings of a woman in Early Indian-Islamic society as opposed to the perception which is commonly held by both religious scholars as well as social scientists that women were oppressed or unable to express their emotions.

The element of representation of these emotions themselves is opposed to this understanding. However, a question can be raised regarding the ambit of emotional expression and the view of a woman as rational.

Another element of the Islamic nature of poetry is that it uses various similes from nature to describe the beloved, this was seen at the zenith of the Ghazal writing and composition seen in the 17th and 18th centuries. A distinctive style of Islamic courtly and spiritual poetry is that of the Rubai.

The form of the Rubai is almost synonymous with Umar Khayyam and Bulleh Shah. However, the origins of the rubai itself are seen to have more ancient roots, it explores the questions about life and divinity in the form of four-lined stanzas. A common theme of rubaiyat was to present the day as an opportunity for self-improvement.

These styles of Islamic poetry were the indigenous form of the Chaupai or four-line poetry common in regional languages such as Awadhi and Hindawi.

Case Study 2: the Ghazals of Amir Khusro

Though it is difficult to pinpoint the exact year in which these Ghazals were composed, linguists who have studied in great detail the works of Amir Khusro, point towards a matured and persianised style of writing, pointing to a more mature and experienced writer in Khusro. This section is divided into two subsections, indicating a closer look at two important ghazals.

> *(a) Ghazal 1836:* figuring as Ghazal 1836, in his Masnawi the Ghazal is divided into two ashar (plural sher) poems. He talks about the idea of how the birth of Khwaja Nizamuddin Auliya is seen as the coming of spring, a full physical description of Nizamuddin Auliya and his mother

is given in this Ghazal. His mother is described to have clear skin and curly hair, not too tall nor too short, living in the region of Namak Cheen, a salt market on a salt trading route from Ajmer to Balkh in the middle East.

Nizamuddin Auliya is also said to have shared his mother's physical looks. However, he had the foresight and wisdom of an older man, even at an early age. This is expressed in the following lines:

"Zehaal-e-miskeen makun taghaful,

Duraye naina banaye batiyan."

Translated, he draws attention to the aspect of the misery of Amir Khusro and requests his Khwaja to not overlook the misery. Another aspect is that he draws attention to the misery of poverty experienced by the Shah himself. He also draws attention to the devotion of Mai Sahiba, when he discusses the idea of patience and her desire to find communion with the divine as discussed in the lines seen below:

" *Ke taab-e-hijran nadaram ay Jaan,*

Na leho kahe lagaye chatiyan."

In the last parts of this Ghazal, Amir Khusro discusses the idea of how this communion with the divine was like awaiting the end of a long Translatingnight. This is depicted in the following lines

"Sakhi Piya ko jo main na dekhun,

To Kaise kaTun andheri ratiyan.

Na nind Naina na ang chaina,

Na aap aaven na bhejen patiyan,"

There, however, is a debate whether, Amir Khusro wrote in honor of Mai Sahiba Bibi Zuekha, as there is no written evidence, however, the Muftis of Nizamuddin Auliya's Dargah hold this belief as these Ghazals are more correspondent to the shringar rasa in nature.

(b) Guftam ke Roshan ke Rozaz Qamar: in this particular Ghazal, Amir khusro does not pay tribute to Mai Sahiba, he, however, pays a tribute to the divine. He questions the listener, about what is more, beautiful than the moon, and the listener responds that it is the cheeks of his beloved (Sanam, God) in the second Stanza, Amir Khusro asks what is sweeter than sugar, to which the listener responds, commands of the divine and the names of God. In the subsequent, he describes the unchanging

and constant nature of his love for Sanam. Two lines from the Ghazal have been reproduced below:

"Guftam Ke Roshan Az Qamar Gufta Ke Rukhsar e Manst

Guftan Ke Shereen Az Shakar Gufta Ke Guftar e Manst"

Case Study 3: Chaap Tilak

The Qawwali Chaap Tilak is probably one of the most popularly performed and remembered. Written in Brij Bjasga to have popular appeal, it is one of Amir Khusro's early Qawwali compositions, depicting the union of the individual with the divine under the able guidance of his Murshid Khwaja Nizamuddin Auliya.

"तन मज तन मन धन बाजी लागी रे

धन धन मोरे भाग बाजी लागी रे

लागी लागी सब कहें

लागी

लागी

लागी

लागी लागी सब कहें

लागी लगी ना अंग

लागी तो जब जानिए

जब रहे गुरु के संग

मौला

ओ जी मौला"

In the First Stanza reproduced below, Amir Khusro talks about how to Unite with the divine, the devotee often needs to gamble away his wealth, business, *and identity.*

"ख़ुसरो रैन सुहाग की

ख़ुसरो रैन सुहाग की

जो मैं जोगी पी के संग

ख़ुसरो बाजी प्रेम की

ख़ुसरो बाजी प्रेम की

जो मैं खेली पी के संग

जीत गयी तो पिया मोरे

जो मैं हारी पी के संग"

In the second stanza of this composition, Amir Khusro discusses how the fortunes of the devotee are connected with the grace of God, similar to how the fortunes of a bride are connected with those of her husband. This reflects the adoption of the female voice in Qawwali music.

" छाप तिलक सब छीन ली रे

मोसे नैना मिलाइके

छाप तिलक सब छीन ली रे

मोसे नैना मिलाइके

छाप तिलक सब छीन ली रे

मोसे नैना मिलाइके

In the third and fourth stanzas of the composition, Amir Khusro, says that in the journey from the Profane to the sacred, an individual loses his identity, arrogance, and pride in himself. He thus describes the activity of Fanah or loss of perception of time and identity which came to be developed in the contemporary urban society.

This can be treated as a socio-political commentary on the state and Sufi relations, where Khusro tends to provide commentary on the nature of devotion that must be displayed instead of the amount of economic endowment.

He points out that in the eyes of God, the markers of social prestige and status are wiped away, revealing the true intent of the individual, therefore, the Sufi endowment cannot in his opinion be used as a source of legitimization for the Sultans. However, this practice continued into the Mughal period.

मोसे नैनान मिलाइके

मोसे बोलो ना बोल

मोसे बोलो ना बोल

मोसे बोलो ना

मोसे बोलो ना

मोसे बोलो ना बोल

मेरी सुन या ना सुन

मैं तो तोहे न चाटूँगी ऐ सावरे

मोसे नैना मिलाइके"

The repetition of the lines of the couplet emphasizes the emotion they portray, further, it provides a rhythmic basis for the highest part of the ending of the Qawwali known as the Tihai, or the threefold repetition of the chorus. In the last part of the last stanza, he alludes to the mystic nature of Sufi knowledge, where he talks about the disappearing path to the divine. Khusro here, emphasizes that the process of Fannah into the divine can be guided by the knowledge of the Pir and the extensive practice of meditation, however, it cannot be seen as an absolute process, but rather is an individual journey, therefore, he alludes to the disappearing footprints, so no other individual can follow his journey.

Case Study 4: Ae Ri Sakhi

The couplet Ae Ri Sakhi is considered to be one of Khusro's last known couplets. Linguists date it to approximately the death of Khwaja Nizamuddin Auliya and Khusro's eath. He describes the scene of a marriage ceremony. Amir Khusro celebrates the coming of his beloved in the first stanza. He discusses the mounting excitement as the marriage procession approaches the courtyard that is decorated.

" ऐ री सखी मोरे पिया घर आए

ऐ री सखी मोरे पिया घर आए

भाग लगे इस आँगन को

भाग लगे इस आँगन को

अपने पिया के मैं बल बल जाऊँ

अपने पिया के मैं बल बल जाऊँ

चरन लगायो निर्धन को

चरन लगायो निर्धन को

ऐ री सखी मोरे पिया घर आए

ऐ री सखी मोरे"

In the second stanza, Amir Khusro talks about a bride standing on the porch of her house, hoping for the arrival of her beloved. She is dressed in a complete ceremonial wedding outfit, Henna to decorate her palms, kohl pencil on her eyes, and vermillion in her hair. These are traditional ornaments worn by married Hindu women to symbolize their status. By using this imagery, Khusro increases the popularity of his work. He also plays with the notion of the death of a Pir being celebrated as a wedding with the divine rather than seeing the occasion as one to be lamented or mourned.

The expectation and excitement are palpable in the writing of Amir Khusro in the last two stanzas of the composition:

" मेंहदी कजरा माँग सजाए

देखी सुरतियां अपने पिया की

देखी सुरतियां अपने पिया की

हार गई मैं तन मन को

हार गई मैं तन मन को

ऐ री सखी मोरे पिया घर आए

जिस के पिया संग बीते सावन

उस दुल्हन की रैन सुहागन

Continuing in the female voice, Amir Khusro adopts the traditional Hindu symbols of Marriage, pointing to the syncretic nature of Sufi-Islam in assimilating the Hindu and Muslim, into a composite Sufi tradition, which was understood and appreciated by the local population. This adoption of various symbols can be seen as an element of the Beshara ruling in the Chishti order that was further strengthened by the understanding of Music and dancing to find a path to the divine.

जिस के पिया संग बीते सावन

उस दुल्हन की रैन सुहागन

जिस सावन में पिया घर नाही

जिस सावन में पिया घर नाही

आग लगे उस सावन को

आग लगे उस सावन को

ऐ री सखी मोरे पिया घर आए"

Amir Khusro has left a lasting impact on the Qawwali form of music, as a popular form. In the modern-day, filmmakers and music in movies. AR Rehman is specifically influenced by the Qawwali style of music. In the Movie, Rockstar, Rehman took inspiration from the ideas of Amir Khusro and developed the chartbuster hit, Kun Faya Kun. Translating to God thought it and it was, it encapsulates the creation myth. AR Rehman invokes the love of God, by talking bout his universality, taking into consideration the lines:

" *Woh jo mujh mein Samaya, Woh jo tujh mein Samaya Maula, wahi wahi Maya*"

Roughly translated, these lines, talk of the spirit of God that is embedded in all of humankind, binding magic. He also includes the aspect of zikr, with chants, taken directly from the Quran, included at various interstices, within the music.

However, it was in the 1950s, that Qawwali was depicted in a movie. It was in the hands of Naushad and Shakeel Badauni in Mughal-e-Azam's famous Teri Mehfil Mein Kismat Azmakar Hum Bhi Dekhengein, that Qawwali gained national repute and stepped out of the traditional regions of Lucknow, Delhi, and Agra. Since then it has been remixed and refreshed in light of new music trends to make it relevant and exciting.

Another popular tune of Amir Khusro is associated with the onset of Spring, especially in the region of the Dargah itself, this song is composed as a bhajan, it invokes the beauty of youth and flowering plants which personify spring. The story behind the development of this composition is well known as a tribute to Nizamuddin Auliya and a request for him to forget the grief of losing a young nephew, instead of embracing the life of the Khanqah and resuming its activities.

In the first stanza of the song, he points out the joy in new life sprouting from the Mustard plant, with the lines *"Sakal ban Phool Rahi Sarson'* Khusro states that the flowers encapsulate the anticipation of various Murids to be blessed once again by their pir, the anticipation of seeing him once would fulfill their anticipation. In the second stanza, he says that people from all walks of life come together at the Khanqah ' *Tarah Tarah ke Phool Lagaye, le Gadhwa Haathan mein Aaye*"

They may be from different walks of life, however, as Amir Khusro points out they are united by their passion for the Pir. He also attempts through this line to point out that Death at any age is a universal fact and therefore, it must not be treated with grief, but rather be celebrated as a union with the beloved (Sanam).

He here points to the Sufi practice of celebrating the death anniversary as Urs. In the last stanza, Amir Khusro points out that all the joy and all the followers of the Pir are at his door. *Nizamuddin kay darwazay par*

Aawan Keh Gaye aashaq rung

Amir Khusro points out that the recent events of the Khanqah, were like the passing seasons, they brought with their sorrow and grief, however, must be left in the past and not be carried into the new year and season that has been brought.

Aur beet Gaye Barson

Malaniyan gadhwa lay aayin Karson

In the last two lines of the Qawwali, Khusro treats the seasons of grief and sorrow as passers-by, and points to the joy brought by the Spring, it to him looks like a young maiden getting dressed to meet her beloved and alluring him out of his shelter, with her beauty and grace. While a large number of Khusro's poems and Qawwalis survived, many were buried with him in letters to his Pir as per his instruction, therefore have been lost.

The of Many Masnavis: Amir Khusro and other Contemporary works

Amir Khusrao has always been celebrated for his literary innovations and one of them are the Masnavis. He took mythological and romantic tales as the subject matter of his narrative verses. Even though Amir khusro's work provides a lot of information to historians of the sultanate period, they tend to be neglected by literary critics because they all defy the established typologies of form and genre in classical Persian literature.

Amir Khusro's Perspective on Astrology

Amir Khusro was the disciple of Khwaja Nizamuddin Auliy, a Chishti saint. Khusrau, himself was famous as a historian, poet, and the originator of Qawwali. However, the themes of Astrology run throughout his poems and Qawwalis.as Shakeel Hossain, mentions that

"Khusrao used elements of astronomy in his poetry in various forms- poetically describing complete horoscopes, through the use of planets, stars and astrological symbolism as metaphors to embellish his historical poems"

Amir Khusrau expresses an entire horoscope in his book Ijaz-i-Khusrawi, Nuh Sipihr, and the Tughlaq Nama. He aimed to adopt a more scientific approach to astrology, similar to that of Hinduism. Khusrau's astrological chart in the form of poems was termed as Zaicha, according to Professor IH Siddiqui, these poems were written on special occasions, for example on the coronation of new Sultans, or the changing of dynasties to predict their future. He takes the example of Munis al Ahrar di daqa'iq, where Khusrau used the various signs of the zodiac to bless the new sultan, with different powers.

He then went on to poetically draw the horoscope at the birth of Prince Muhammad, the son of Qutubuddin Mubarak Shah, Khusrau went on to describe the relevance of all 12 signs of the zodiac on the natal chart. In another masnavi, he provided the horoscope of Princess Dewal Devi of Gujarat. To make his work more credible, Khusrau used an Astrolabe, that was similar to the large sundials, constructed at Jantar Mantar. He also

aided the usage and designing of the celestial globes, to

map the movement of zodiac signs.

A Closer Examination of Four Masnavis

LAILA MAJNUN

Romance is unique in Persian literature in more than one respect. First, it's a theme; second, it belongs to the domain of history beyond mythology; thirdly it describes India's culture. Some scholars in the earliest stages of their research were based in Europe as was the case in most Asian, Middle Eastern Heritage and historical studies. They likened the story of Laila and Majhnu to the stories of Romeo and Juliet, one of forbidden love. This aspect and idea were taken up by Hindi and Urdu scholars to liken this aspect with the ideals of Sufi literature and the iconic Prem Akhyan texts.

The story, similar to the story of Chandayan, revolves around primarily, two characters, Laila and Majhnu. Majhnu is depicted in the 9th and 10th centuries as part of the Early Arabic Sufi tradition, Kitab al Shir wa al Shu'ara, dating to the Umayyad period of the late ninth century. Krachovski, in her research, uses the reference of Majhnu to explain the character of a Sufi disciple, enraged with the love of the divine. Earlier, depictions, are said to have dehumanized Majhnu, treating him as an imaginary, ill-fated lover. He was also considered to be bereft of all emotions and feelings, thus, being a reflection of all the negative practices depicted within Islam. To Ritter, Majhnu's single-minded focus and devotion towards attaining his love, Laila, sets him apart from contemporaneous characters such as Laurik.

Laila is considered to be the depiction of the divine, similar to Chanda. Laila, similar to Laurik is married off to the son of a wealthy Bedouin Chief, upon the death of her husband, she rejoices as it symbolizes the beginning of her union with her lover, Majhnu.

This is a similar depiction to that of the Chandayan. However, the Chandayan ends with the untimely death of the two young lovers. This Masnavi is said to have a Happy Ending, with both Laila and Majhnu, being depicted as martyrs in love. Another view placed on the text is that Laila o Majhnu is a didactic text, that portrays the various stages of the union with the divine.

This, however, does not reduce its romantic character, but rather enhances it in the light of divine love. Laila and Majhnu are buried together, as a symbol of eternal love. Amir Khusro highlights the romantic nature of their relationship, he, however, aims to portray a physical relationship, as opposed to a spiritual one as depicted by his predecessors. His work is a synthesis of the traditions of the Indic-Persian style, by the usage of hybrid languages. Subsequently, the Mughal, Ottoman, and Safavid versions of the story overtook the Sultanat period metaphor of Majhnu mourning over the grave of Laila.

The story of Laila and Majhnu is said to be the basis of the later Sufi texts, such as Heer-Ranjha as composed by Bulle Shah popularly known as Bullah in the 17th and

18th centuries. His poems were based on the principles of self-obliteration given to the master.

Set in the foothills of Punjab, the story of Heer-Ranjha originally composed by Waris Shah, Ranjha abandons his home and responsibilities in search of Heer, the daughter of a local pastoral chieftain who hires Ranjha as a herdsman, thus, providing the opportunity for Heer and Ranjha to Interact. Bulle Shah, ornamented this poem with simple and lucid metaphors, to throw light on the relationship of Sufi love.

This lucid style of writing affected the style of Waris Shah, who is known for his work, Qissa Waris Shah, often considered a raw portrayal of emotions and emulated in several forgeries (11609 forged verses).

His memory was immortalized by Amrita Pritam, in her moving poem Aaj Akhan Waris Shah Nun. Translated to today, in the land of Waris Shah. She evoked the spirit of these Sufis to depict the plight of an embattled Punjab and struggling women, in light of Partition.

ASHIQA (DEWAL RANI – KHIZR KHAN)

The Ashiqa is sometimes referred to as the 3rd Masnavi composed by khusrau and was completed around 1313AD. The central theme of the poem is the romance and the tragic fate of Khizr Khan, son of Sultan Alauddin Khilji, and the princess Dewal Rani daughter of Karan Deva II of Gujarat. Here Amir Khusrao had tried to incorporate the symbolic union of the two civilizations- Hindu and Muslim.

For the Prince love mattered more than anything else. The conflict was a natural outcome of it. The result of this love affair was celebrated with manuscripts of Ashiqa appearing in Indian history from time to time. So many fabricated stories exist about this episode, that none is reliable. Due to the unfortunate death of Khizr khan as a prisoner, he updated the Masnavi with a tragic end.

TUGHLAQ NAMA

Amir Khusrau wrote his last Masnavi the Tughlaq Nama in which he chronicled all the expeditions which had led to the murder of king Qutbuddin Khilji by khusrau Khan. It also deals with the short-lived period of khusrau Khan's rule in Delhi. This preamble describes the Great War that was fought between the army of Ghiyasuddin Tughlaq and khusrau Khan near Delhi in which the army of khusrau Khan was routed and he was subsequently killed. the poem is full of religiopolitical fervor it lacks in Epic magnitude.

For a long time, it was believed that this work was lost but later on the lost fragments of the Masnavi were compiled with the preface and conclusion by Hayati.

NUH SAPHIR

The famous Sufi poet, Amir Khusrau wrote a Masnavi on the Tughlaq dynasty ruler, Mubarak Shah as \"Nuh Sipihr" (Nine Skies), relating the events of Mubarak Shah\'s rule.

He categories his poem into 9 sections or chapters, for each part is deliberated as a sky.

The introduction contains beautiful verses dedicated to Hazrat Nizamuddin Auliya.

In the 3rd section of this Masnavi, he composed an intense explanation of India and its surroundings, seasons, vegetation and wildlife, philosophies, sciences, ethos, traditions, researchers, etc. he chronicled all the conquest and the achievements that Sultan Qutbuddin Shah had made in the early years of his reign and has presented many aspects of the Indian culture as mentioned above. Along with that of music and horoscope of his son in this Masnavi. This Masnavi is and is a great piece as it provides information beyond his interest in poetry, music, etc.

CHANDAYAN: A DETAILED OVERVIEW

Popularly known as Laur Chanda, this text was composed by Mulla Daud, it was one of the texts that formed the backbone of the Prem Akhyan texts. To Dr. BN Goswamy, it has a lasting impact on the reader due to its local appeal and intricate Persian sophistication. The story is set in several Karwaks, or short poem style writing in a fusion of Persianate and Indian languages such as Awadhi, pointing towards the larger vernacularization of Persian writing, seen in a pure form in Malfuzat texts. In this text, the reader sees glimpses, of an interplay between Sufi mysticism and astronomy.

The epic revolves around three principal characters, each representing either an astronomical entity or a devotional emotion. Lorik (often spelled as Laurik), is the representation of the Sun, here the Sun, is said to be the divine light of Sufism. Chanda, the daughter of a local ruler is considered, to be the representation of the Moon. She falls in love with Laurik as an outcome.

The epic starts, with the birth of Chanda, here, we see, astrologers, reading her horoscope and predicting her death, at the prime of her youth.

 As a result of this separation by death, both Laurik and Chanda die, representing urs, the marriage of the divine and the Sufi. The third character is Maina, the wife of Laurik, who is depicted as the representation of mainstream society. Maina is portrayed in deep sorrow on the 'loss of her husband, she thus represents the rejection of the orthodox practices towards the way of the Sufi.

Mulla Daud also incorporates the idea of reconciliation between the Sufis and the Ulama, through the depiction of the return of Laur-Chanda to Lorik's marital home. This is more ways than one, was a political commentary on the relations of the state represented by Maina and the Sufis represented by the love of Lorik and Chanda. As NR Farooqi highlights, the initially strained relations of the Sufis and state, which also extended to a certain degree in the mature part of the sultanate, eased towards its decline.

Other Impacts of Amir Khusro's Work: A Collection of Miscellany

Amir Khusro was known for his ability as a poet, a musician, Sufi, an astrologer, and a Historian. A man who in his life wore many hats and for some may have like Da Vinci in the future, idealized a Renaissance man, filled with the curiosity and knowledge of various disciplines.

He lives on in the minds of young children even to this day, though, they do not know it, the riddles children solved were often challenges of court entertainment. There are many such riddles popularly associated with Amir Khusro. However, two interesting ones include: " Aisi Konsi tokri Hai, jo Sar par sath Chalti hai, par agar giro, toh usmein se Ek moti Nahi girta?" translated, this riddle would mean," which basket is such, that it moves on our heads, but if we fall, no a single pearl is seen to fall outside of this basket?"

The answer is the night sky, which is filled with pearls. The metaphor of Pearls is seen to describe the stars and other celestial objects. Centuries later, scholars would identify a similar trend of Sufism, being reflected in the Adi Granth of the Guru Granth Sahib, sacred to the Sikhs. In the couplet, Aqeedat e Sartaj, the First Guru, Guru Nanak, is said to have been attending an arti (prayer) at the temple of Jagannath Puri, when he witnessed some people of a lower caste being discriminated against.

He refused to join in the Arti and composed the tune of his own Arti path, which saw the Skies as the Thal (prayer tray), this idea of Celestial objects symbolizing the divine along with their universality, can be seen in the Bhakti traditions of Hinduism, a phenomenon, parallel to the Sufi movement in the subcontinent.

This is evident in the Alvar sect of the Bhaktas, who used the beauty of the moon to describe the calm nature and physical beauty of Lord Krishna. The hymn was popularised by Kishori Amonkar, in the 1960s, by the name Saguna Sarupa Nand Lal. set in Raga Chandrakauns, it evokes natural beauty and attraction to the divine as experienced by Mirabai.

Though, from diverse periods and faiths, the idea of the sky being as universal as God, Nirgun, or Saguna and impartial is a constant factor in mainstream devotional practices. Amir Khusro also goes on to throw light on the lifestyle and food habits of the local elite of the Delhi Sultanate. He describes people, to have a fairly common and well-established practice of travel.

This is an activity, he too, is seen to be indulging in. In the process of his wide travels, Amir Khusro, depicts the natural climate of India, as conducive to the development of orchards of the fruit of a large variety. Being, from the colder region of Central Asia, Khusro describes India to be in a perpetual season of spring.

He describes, the agricultural abundance found in India, along with exotic species along with Peacock and Peafowl. . In the third season of the Nuh Saphir, Khusro vividly depicts the flora and fauna of India. He describes the air to be laden with the scent of mango, Cardamom, camphor, and Cloves.

The seasons in India are described to be mild and even-tempered. This leads to a varying number of dishes at Banquets, owing to a temperate and pleasant climate, leading to abundance. Khusro describes 42 different types of menu items at royal banquets. The common features include Sambusa (a meat-filled Samosa), Qurs (thin flat bread), and nan tanuri (an early version of fermented nan). When describing sweet meets, Khusro describes Kak, a favorite of Qutubuddin Bakhtiar Kaki, Halwa, and Almond Marzipan (commonly enjoyed today as Burfi).

In another riddle, Khusro describes the ending of a meal " what is green when you eat it but red when it is expelled?" The answer to his riddle is paan or betel leaf, which was identified by Khusro with 42 benefits. His detailed account also seems to have influenced the accounts of Ibn Batuta, Nicolo Conti, and Al biruni, as all of them describe the vibrant market places, and variety of food and Ibn Batuta describes paan as peculiarly grown primarily for people to chew on and expel.

The Mughals also threw light on the diverse topographical conditions of India and the richness of native fruit plants, in their personal memoirs that may have been influenced by their observations and the writings of Khusro.

Epilogue

The Relevance of Amir Khusro can be seen in a socio-cultural context as the outcome of an interaction between the Turks and the native element as suggested by Mehru Jaffer. His footprint, however, is more predominant an element, as it provides a narrative counter to the court narrative of historical recollection in the Sultanate period.

A historian contemporary to the times of Amir Khusro was Ziauddin Barani, in his writings, Ziauddin Barani emphasizes the pedigree of the historian himself rather than the level of accuracy as seen in the work. He states that a historian must be of noble and high birth to better understand the nuances of historical writing and the nature of sources, which must be handled with care. He deals, however, with sources rather callously in the writing of his own texts.

Professor Ishtiyaq Ahmad Zilli highlights that the writing of the Tarikh-i-Firozshahi was written while the author was imprisoned and therefore, resulted in a reliance on Memory. He also highlights that the writing of Barani was state-sponsored and therefore, reliant on state patronage, and thus was extended while in praise of the Sultan and his policies.

On the contrary, the writings of Amir Khusro were based on the lived experiences of those whom he saw and interacted with at the Majlis of the Khanqah.

The writings of Khusro also highlight the composite nature of social interactions, which focuses on the similarities between the native and Islamic traditions. He aimed at reconstructing the Historical tradition of the

Khanqah itself, his writings held within it the element of oral narrative records and foreign perspectives. The interaction of the diverse cultures also seems to reflect in the linguistic choices of Amir Khusro as he is popularly viewed for the development of Hindawi as a dialect.

It has been held by Sheldon Pollock that there was a connection between the high and the low languages, which were the Vernacular languages that developed as a medley of several elite languages. In the case of Hindawi, it is a combination of Arabic, Persian, Sanskrit, Turkish, Braj Bhasha, and Khari Boli, a native form of Sanskrit, in the absence of the multiple tonal graces and grammatical practices.

To Francesca Orsini further, the development of Hindawi was instrumental in the writing of history as a multi-cultural and multi-lingual interaction.

Hindawi further developed in the writing of Historian and poet Amir Khusro, who developed the language that incorporated the graces of the dialect Awadhi, which had been used by composers in earlier decades as the basis of historical writing due to the rhythmic nature of the language.

Linguistically speaking, the language of Awadh, along with Braja Bhasha are softer languages as compared to Arabic and Persian which are heavily reliant on the epiglottis of the speaker.

These languages are softer as they have a rounded and poetic sound, thus lending themselves with ease to the writing of Chaupai, Ghazal, and Rubai. However, due to its soft character, the language came to become common currency between the composers of Masnavi and Prem Akhyan texts, borrowing from the Bardic traditions of the Gangetic plain. Further, the language underwent multiple changes before being accepted as a form of writing by the Mughal nobility and elite during the reign of Akbar. Hindawi is said to have reached its zenith of development as reflected in the writings of Faizi, the brother of Abul Fazl and Abdur Rahim Khan- Khanan. A work brought into the limelight by Faizi was the Masnavi Ashiqa, the story of Nal and Damyanti, the text was seen to have a typical Gujarati influence, with the development of the landscapes and the dialect.

On the contrary, the writing of the Ashiqa by Amir Khusro was more classical in its rendition, the Ashiqa was reliant on more Islamic backdrops, while the language of choice was proto-Hindawi still rooted heavily in the Turkish language as seen by linguistic historians. This form of the Ashiqa blended with the

Gujarati form of the Ashiqa and is combined today to develop the nature of the Ashiqa recounted by modern Dastango traditions. However, it was in the Doha writing tradition of Rahim, that this element of Proto-Hindawi was preserved and shares similarities with the writings of Khusro and Kabir.

Due to the borrowed nature of the Soft expressive language as pointed out by Mughlis, Hindawi has gained an appeal among many, young and old, to this day.

Socio-Economic and Political Impacts of Sufism in India

Sufism was and continues to be an important social force in modern India. Today, more and more people identify themselves with a universal religion or agnostic, to distinguish themselves from the orthodox hardliners. Socially speaking, Sufism is treated by the Indian government as an extension of Islam. It is considered a minority practice under the broader aegis of the religion. Sufism has been a vehicle of change since its inception, it provides for social formations based on love, peace, and harmony. Sufism has played an important role in the acceptance of Islam by broader society.

Initially, Islam spread only in the region of Sindh and Multan, due to the interaction and settlement of Muslims from Central Asia and the Middle East. Sufism entered India in the 12th century with Khwaja Moinuddin Chishti. Sufism, in its fold, amalgamated the Hindu and Islamic traditions, which led to the proliferation of Islam within the sub-continent. The Qadiriyya sect of the Sufis in India led to the development of Islamic proliferation in India. This is because to be accepted under a Murshid one needed to convert.

Further, Sufism also led to social reform within Islam. The Aligarh Movement, under the leadership of Sir Syed Ahmad Khan in the 17th century, introduced scientific temper within the broader fold of Islam. Further, the ruling classes were encouraged to pursue a more tolerant and diverse policy towards various sects, thus, leading to a reduction in wars and riots against the nobility and ruling class.

Politically speaking, Sufism and the state had various types of relationships, that changed over time. Initially, the Sufi saints maintained a distance from the state and its machinery. This implied that the Sufi Khanqah was seen as a mutually exclusive zone, a place where the state could not interfere to extract taxes or impose upon it to gain legitimacy.

However, under Nizamuddin Auliya, the nature of the Sufi Khanqah changed dramatically, he chose as his successor, Amir Khusro, a Turkoman noble, who held many important positions, with the court of the Ilbari,

Khilji, and Tughlaq rulers. He was appointed to the court in the position of astrologer, poet, and a small-scale iqtadar. However, the Pir and the Sultan maintained a distance. A story goes, that upon hearing that Jalaluddin Khalji was coming to meet him, from Amir Khusro, Khwaja Nizamuddin Auliya left the Khanqah from the back for a ziarat to Ajodhan, at the shrine of Baba Farid Ganj I Shakar.

In the period of the Delhi Sultanate, under Muhammad Bin tughlaq and Ghyasuddin Balban, the Sufis and the state had a confrontational relationship, scholars have uncovered how, the ruling elite granted lands and charitable donations to the Sufis, however, later revoked of demanded the payment of taxes. However, Nizamuddin Chirag i Delhalvi, opposed the repayment of state dues, throwing light on the aspect that the endowments were gifts from the state, not solicited by trade or commerce.

Under the Mughal rule, scholars trace ties between the ruling class, and the location of Dargah was central to city organization. especially, the position of graves and tombs close to the Pirs was seen as an important aspect of honoring the dead. This tradition was established with the construction of Humayun's tomb, the first Islamic tomb to be built in India, which is currently located opposite the Dargah of Khwaja Nizamuddin Auliya. Humayun's tomb is a complex of tombs, constructed under the able guidance of Hajji begum, who rests close to her husband's grave.

The tomb within it is a reflection of Sufi ideals as it is a blend of Indian and Arabic motifs, and Islamic philosophical beliefs and is at a sacred place at the feet of Nizamuddin Auliya. Further, in this locality, one can also observe the tombs of Adgah Khan and Jiji Anga, the foster parents and regents of Akbar, who was the leader of the Adgah Khail, a family loyal to the Emperor. However, the tombs of Maham Anga and Adham Khan are distant from any Dargah, as they were labeled traitors and though, buried were not rewarded for their services.

Akbar is said to have visited the Khanqah of Salim Chishti, six times, his son, Prince Salim, was considered a blessing from the Pir. As a mark of respect, Akbar donated the Degh, a vessel to cook Khichdi as part of the Langar. Jahangir also is considered to be a patron of

Sufism, patronizing the Sufi sect of Kashmir, Ajodhan, and Ajmer along with Jhulelal of Sindh (Lahore) and Nizamuddin Auliya of Delhi. Shah Jahan, also like his grandfather was a patron of the Chishti Silsila, he is recorded to have traveled multiple times to the Dargah of Moinuddin Chishti. It was art Historian Milo C Beach, who draws the attention of historians to the existence of a painting in which his horse is blinded by the appearance of Moinuddin Chishti's Spirit. This painting (reproduced below), from the Padshahnama collection of the Windsor Castle, shows the emphasis on the tie with Sufis. This was a tool of gain legitimacy.

The associations of the Sufis, in the court of Shah Jahan, do not end with the emphasis on the Chishti order. His wazir, Chandrabhan Brahmin, is also said to have pledged his loyalty to the Chishti sect, he also trained Dara Shikoh and begum Nadira, Dara Shikoh's wife. They traveled to the hills of the Kashmir valley, as recorded by Supriya Gandhi and Rajiv Kinra. Shah Jahan's daughter, Jahanara, was also considered a Fakira, though loyal to the Qadri sect of Sufism, she is buried closest to the grave of Nizamuddin Auliya, between him and Amir Khusro. Later Mughals such as Muhammad Shah (rangeela), Akbar Shah, and others, are buried near the shrine of Nizamuddin Auliya.

During the period of British rule in India, the policy of divide and rule made Dargahs and Mosques, symbolize fear for non-muslims and symbolize a safe haven for Muslims in Hindu or Sikh-dominated areas. These differences became sharper, after the Government of

India Act 1937, 1942, which provided for separate electorates for Hindus and Muslims. A moderate wing of Indian politicians and Freedom fighters continued to sue for a non-violent partition or the reunion of India. Maulana Abdul Kalam Azad used the Jama Masjid as a symbol of religious and political unity and appealed to the basic tenets of brotherhood to adopt the methods of peace and tolerance between individuals from different faiths.

However, it was Mahatma Gandhi, who in the course of his final fast unto death in 1948, used the ideals of Sufism and tolerance to prevent bloodshed. As Khushwant Singh records, it was 27th January 1948, a cold and misty day in the national capital. To communicate a message of tolerance and brotherhood,

Mahatma Gandhi, stayed at the Valmiki colony in the locality and taught their children at the local school, providing kar seva at the local shrine.

He addressed the locals from the Dargah of Qutubuddin Bakhtiar Kaki, with the basic tenets of Islam and Sufism. Mahatma Gandhi also visited the local Yog Maya temple to spread a message of equality and respect for his quest. However, in the subsequent days, Mahatma Gandhi was assassinated by Nathuram Godse.

Throughout the twentieth and twenty-first centuries, sacred shrines of the Sufis are primary places of political activity and address, especially on the campaign route. Each Prime Minister of India, after election generally visits a Dargah (generally Ajmer), one of the four

Mathas and the Golden Temple, to seek the blessings of all the deities, by whose grace, they are seen to be elected.

On the question of Economy and the Economic relevance of shrines and places of worship, scholars generally see the rise of commercial centers, haats, or markets in the vicinity. The presence of a Dargah is the lifeline to many florists, who sell incense sticks, chadars, and other offerings for the saint.

Though these individuals are categorized as self-employed and earn from a respectable job, they are in the below taxation bracket. Therefore, they do not appear to contribute to the GDP, their income is unstable and fluctuates from very high at the time of urs and very low to unemployment in the case of a disaster such as the COVID-19 Pandemic. Due to lesser footfalls at shrines, owing to the COVID-19 restrictions, many florists, food carts, and drinks vendors find themselves struggling, having to migrate from one place to another in search of stable employment.

References

Eaton, Richard M. India in the Persianate Age, Print

Chittick, William C. Sufism. Simon and Schuster, 2007.

Dehalvi,Sadia, Sufism: The Heart of Islam. Print.

Schimmel, Anne Marie Sufism: the Mystic Dimension of Islam.

Dehlavi, Sadia. Delhi: the Sufi Courtyard Print.

Nasir, Rabia. Role and Importance of Sufism in the Modern World.

Ernst, Carl W. Sufism. Shambhala Publications, 2017.

Rizvi, Saiyid Athar Abbas. "A history of Sufism in India." (1978).

Raziuddin Aquil; 2018, Hazrat-i-Dehli: The Making of the Chishti Sufi Centre and the

Stronghold of Islam

Jonali Sarma; 2020, The Socio-Economic condition of 13th- 14th Century Medieval India and

the role played by Sufi Saints for improvement in livelihood conditions of the Sultanate

Shah, Bullhe. Sufi Lyrics. Harvard University Press, 2021.

Aquil, Raziuddin. Days in the Life of a Sufi. PanMacmillan, 2020

Thapar, Romila. The Past Before Us. Harvard University Press, 2013.

Kumar, Sunil. The Emergence of the Delhi Sultanate, 1192-1286. 2010.

Shahab, Syed Yusuf. The Lost Sufis of Delhi. OrangeBooks Publication, 2020.

Armstrong, Karen. Islam. Modern Library, 2007.

Batuta, Ibn. The Travels of Ibn Batūta. 1829.

Tarikh-i-Firozshahi, Ziauddin Barani

Tabqat-i-Nasiri, Minhaj-us-Siraj Juzjani

Khanum Farida, Dr. Origin and Evolution of Sufism

Cook Benjamin G. Understanding Sufism Contextualising the Content

Dey, Dr. Amit , " Muslim mystics and sufi silsilahs in India" 2016, e copy

Dutta, Uttaran, "Sufi and Bhakti Performers and Followers at the Margin of Global South: Communication Strategies to Negotiate Situated Diversities" 2019, e copy

AGAKHAN TRUST FOR CULTURE WORLD OF AMIR KHUSRO

Pollock, Sheldon, Literary Cultures and History: Reconstructions from South Asia, Print

Orsini Francesca, Print And Pleasure: Popular Literature And Entertaining Fictions In Colonial North India, Print

Orsini Francesca, History of the Book in South Asia, Print.

Alam Muzzafar, Language of Political Islam in India, Print.

Parveen, Abida. Aaj Rang Hai. 1 Jan. 2000,

https://audio-ssl.itunes.apple.com/itunes-assets/AudioPre

view115/v4/55/c7/5d/55c75d8d-2267-6

9d4-38ba-bc75980f8b69/mzaf_16328894336042695667.

plus.aac.p.m4a.

Choudhary, Namita. Ae Re Sakhi. 8 Feb. 2021,

https://audio-ssl.itunes.apple.com/itunes-assets/AudioPre

view125/v4/3b/10/ae/3b10ae8f-b83c-e5

32-1793-ae7d0bbaaa92/mzaf_172595469999149365277.p

lus.aac.p.m4a.

Khan, Abida Parveen &. Rahat Fateh Ali. Chaap Tilak.

23 Nov. 2014,

https://audio-ssl.itunes.apple.com/itunes-assets/AudioPre

view125/v4/4d/25/68/4d2568ff-80db-4

2fa-bb2c-236a5ebc5815/mzaf_6270479163518606276.p

lus.aac.p.m4a.

Brothers, Sabri. Zehal-E-Miskeen. 1 Apr. 1987,

https://audio-ssl.itunes.apple.com/itunes-assets/AudioPre

view115/v4/e2/92/6b/e2926b0b-b4b8-4

c36-17d6-7f0f72d4c6fa/mzaf_8277104813659614730.pl

us.aac.p.m4a.

Singh, Satinder, Aqeedat e Sartaj

https://youtu.be/QxEL53vdjmc

206

Kishori Amonkar Mharo Pranam

Amonkar, Kishori. Mharo Pranam. 1 Jan. 1995,

https://audio-ssl.itunes.apple.com/itunes-assets/AudioPre

view115/v4/aa/9d/c6/aa9dc6f3-af1f-211

a-1670-e1574fa53648/mzaf_11761645897247204407.pl

us.aac.p.m4a.

207

Miscellaneous

Amir Khusrau ke Rang- Ankit Chadha

https://youtu.be/zza8bQPmmGE

Festival of Kabir- Dastan-e Kabir

https://youtu.be/DBspbWs6jZg

A Short Movie on Amir Khusro

https://youtu.be/-GLugZitupo

Soulful Kabir Bhajan | Kalaam-e-Kabir with Shabnam

Virmani | Jashn-e-Rekhta

https://youtu.be/wpGOMJP2ges

Aaj Akhan Waris Shah Nu recited by Gulzar

https://youtu.be/RdUl90Mv7d8

Gulzar Saab on Amrita Pritam

https://youtu.be/-4xaRRiJD1A